BEING SAD WHEN SOMEONE DIES

A BOOK ABOUT GRIEF

Written by
Linus Mundy

Illustrated by
Anne FitzGerald

ABBEY PRESS Publications
1 Hill Drive
St. Meinrad, IN 47577

Text © 2012 Linus Mundy
Illustrations © 2012 St. Meinrad Archabbey
Published by Abbey Press Publications
1 Hill Drive
St. Meinrad, Indiana 47577

Library of Congress Catalog Number
2012905191

ISBN 978-0-87029-501-0

Printed in the United States of America.

A Message from the Author
to Parents and Caring Adults

All of life is so precious that we are saddened when any of it ends. When someone we care about dies, we can feel lost, confused, and deeply grieved.

For children, who are "new" at so many things, it can be a very difficult experience to lose a loved one. For the very young, the finality of death is hard to understand. How, after all, could something like this happen? Where is this person? Will they be back? Who is going to take care of me now? The questions and the sadness, whether they are voiced or not, can go on and on.

It is for us to "be there" for these young people going through a loss. They need all the support and concern we can muster. They will work through some of the experience in their own way and in their own time, of course. But we can take them by the hand and share what we know about getting through such a difficult time. We can reassure them that, some way, somehow, things can be good again.

Being Sad When Someone Dies can help you and your grieving child or grandchild or young friend. It attempts to speak not in allegories or story, but directly to the child in words he or she can understand. It offers practical coping skills as well as perhaps a better understanding of the circle of life itself. May the words and pictures in this book bring comfort and support to you and your grieving child.

—*Linus Mundy*

So many feelings.

When someone you love dies, you have so many feelings—feelings that you don't like. You may feel sad. You might also feel a little bit scared, mixed-up, lost, yucky in the stomach, angry, or worried. You may even feel "numb"—no feelings inside, at all—because you are so surprised that this happened.

You might even have all of these feelings at the same time.

Being sad is not being bad.

Some people think they should pretend that nothing bad happened when someone dies. They think that if they don't cry or say or do anything different, maybe things will be better.

But you can't just forget that a person you loved died. Because you loved that person.

We can all help each other.

One good thing that happens when someone you love dies, is that people want to help each other at this time. They want to make the sadness not quite so bad, the badness not quite so sad. They want to be with people who know how they're feeling.

Talking about your feelings.

Talking to a grown-up or a friend can really help with your sad feelings. Your parent or grandparent or teacher might be the best persons to talk with.

Some of the people they have loved have died in the past, and so they know some of the things that can help.

Talking about the person who died.

You may hear people saying nice things about the person who died, and telling stories and maybe even laughing. It is good to remember the good things about this person and to talk about him or her.

You may want to try copying some of the good things this person did. If your loved one had a garden or a special plant, you may want to plant a garden or take care of a plant, too.

God is with you and the person who died.

Our religion teaches us that only a person's body dies. We all have a soul that never dies. Our souls go to heaven to be with God who loves the one who has died as much as you do.

It helps to know this. But it still hurts that our friend or family member died and we can't hug them or talk to them anymore.

Remembering good things helps.

Thinking about the good things you did when the person was alive can help a lot.

Yes, it may make you sad to think that you can't do more good things with that person. But remembering the happy times you had together can make you very glad that this person was alive and shared with you.

Something to help you remember.

Maybe you can ask your mom or dad to get you a reminder of the person who died. It might be a wooden spoon that your grandparent let you use to help cook, or a book that your uncle really liked, or maybe a happy picture of the person that you can frame and put in your room.

Nighttime may be the hardest.

When you are really tired at night, you may have sad thoughts as you lie in bed and everything is quiet.

Remember that even though you are sad now, there will be many happy times ahead. Life will be different, and you will definitely miss this person who died, but God and the people you love will be near you.

Making or doing things can also help.

Maybe you can draw pictures of yourself playing or talking with the person when he or she was alive. Or maybe you can help your mom or dad bake and eat a pie that you used to make together. Or make a scrapbook of drawings and pictures that remind you of how wonderful this person was and the things you did together.

Asking God to help you and everyone.

Some people say that even God is sad when a person dies. It is good to talk with God in prayer. Ask God to help you and your family and friends at this time. Ask God to take good care of the person who died.

In your mind, you can even talk to the person who died. Maybe write a letter saying all the things you are feeling and wish you could tell them.

Going to the cemetery.

If the person's body is buried at a cemetery, you might want to go there with a grown-up and visit the grave. The cemetery is often in a nice, green field with trees and flowers all around.

Seeing these plants and trees is a good reminder that there is a big "circle of life"—flowers bloom and then die and more flowers grow. They are all beautiful and we enjoy them while they are there.

The cemetery is also a good place to remember that people's souls live on forever, with God.

You can help others who are sad.

You bring happiness to all who love you just by being yourself. When someone dies, we all need each other more than ever.

Your friends and family need YOU to be happy again. They want you to keep growing and being the special person that you are.

Giving hugs or just sitting quietly next to someone can help them not to feel so sad.

Miracles.

A "miracle" is something wonderful that only God can make happen.

Life itself is a miracle. One of the greatest miracles is that love goes on forever— just like a person's soul.

Remember that God's love for all of us, including the person who has died, will go on forever. What a miracle!

Linus Mundy has written a number of books for children and grown-ups, as well as articles for the religious press. The founder of the popular *CareNotes* and *CareNotes for Kids* booklet series from Abbey Press, he has written *Slow-down Therapy* and *Keep-life-simple Therapy*, and several books on prayer and spiritual growth. Linus and his wife, Michaelene, wrote the *Bringing Religion Home* newsletter for a number of years.

Anne FitzGerald is an internationally known artist and has written and illustrated over 200 children's books. She is creator of "Dear God Kids" and many other children's books and products. Anne works from her studio/gallery in Limerick, Ireland, and teaches art in Liberty Christian School there.